MY ADVENTURES IN READING

MY ADVENTURES IN READING
BOOK JOURNAL

TITLE :   DATE STARTED :
                                          DATE FINISHED :

AUTHOR :
☐ BIPOC   ☐ AAPI   ☐ LATINX   ☐ ESL   ☐ LGBTQ+
CATEGORY / GENRE :

SO... WHAT'D YOU THINK?

☐ NOT MY BAG   ☐ JUST OK   ☐ TOTALLY RAD!
☐ A REAL SLOG   ☐ REPEAT READ   ☐ THIS BOOK CHANGED
  BUT WORTH IT   FOR SURE   MY LIFE

QUICK SUMMARY / LOGLINE :

QUOTE OR CONCEPT TO REMEMBER :

WHO WOULD YOU RECOMMEND THIS TO :

TITLE :   DATE STARTED :
           DATE FINISHED :

AUTHOR :

☐ BIPOC   ☐ AAPI   ☐ LATINX   ☐ ESL   ☐ LGBTQ+

CATEGORY / GENRE :

SO... WHAT'D YOU THINK?

☐ NOT MY BAG   ☐ JUST OK   ☐ TOTALLY RAD!
☐ A REAL SLOG   ☐ REPEAT READ   ☐ THIS BOOK CHANGED
  BUT WORTH IT   FOR SURE   MY LIFE

QUICK SUMMARY / LOGLINE :

QUOTE OR CONCEPT TO REMEMBER :

WHO WOULD YOU RECOMMEND THIS TO :

TITLE :   DATE STARTED :
                                         DATE FINISHED :

AUTHOR :
☐ BIPOC   ☐ AAPI   ☐ LATINX   ☐ ESL   ☐ LGBTQ+
CATEGORY / GENRE :

SO... WHAT'D YOU THINK?

☐ NOT MY BAG   ☐ JUST OK   ☐ TOTALLY RAD!
☐ A REAL SLOG   ☐ REPEAT READ   ☐ THIS BOOK CHANGED
  BUT WORTH IT   FOR SURE   MY LIFE

QUICK SUMMARY / LOGLINE :

QUOTE OR CONCEPT TO REMEMBER :

WHO WOULD YOU RECOMMEND THIS TO :

TITLE :   DATE STARTED :
                                     DATE FINISHED :

AUTHOR :
☐ BIPOC   ☐ AAPI   ☐ LATINX   ☐ ESL   ☐ LGBTQ+
CATEGORY / GENRE :

SO... WHAT'D YOU THINK?

☐ NOT MY BAG   ☐ JUST OK   ☐ TOTALLY RAD!
☐ A REAL SLOG   ☐ REPEAT READ   ☐ THIS BOOK CHANGED
  BUT WORTH IT   FOR SURE   MY LIFE

QUICK SUMMARY / LOGLINE :

QUOTE OR CONCEPT TO REMEMBER :

WHO WOULD YOU RECOMMEND THIS TO :

TITLE :　　　　　　　　　　DATE STARTED :
　　　　　　　　　　　　　　DATE FINISHED :

AUTHOR :
☐ BIPOC　☐ AAPI　☐ LATINX　☐ ESL　☐ LGBTQ+
CATEGORY / GENRE :

SO... WHAT'D YOU THINK?

☐ NOT MY BAG　　☐ JUST OK　　　　☐ TOTALLY RAD!

☐ A REAL SLOG　　☐ REPEAT READ　　☐ THIS BOOK CHANGED
　BUT WORTH IT　　　FOR SURE　　　　　MY LIFE

QUICK SUMMARY / LOGLINE :

QUOTE OR CONCEPT TO REMEMBER :

WHO WOULD YOU RECOMMEND THIS TO :

TITLE : DATE STARTED :
DATE FINISHED :

AUTHOR :
☐ BIPOC ☐ AAPI ☐ LATINX ☐ ESL ☐ LGBTQ+
CATEGORY / GENRE :

SO... WHAT'D YOU THINK?
☐ NOT MY BAG ☐ JUST OK ☐ TOTALLY RAD!
☐ A REAL SLOG BUT WORTH IT ☐ REPEAT READ FOR SURE ☐ THIS BOOK CHANGED MY LIFE

QUICK SUMMARY / LOGLINE :

QUOTE OR CONCEPT TO REMEMBER :

WHO WOULD YOU RECOMMEND THIS TO :

TITLE : DATE STARTED :
DATE FINISHED :

AUTHOR :
☐ BIPOC ☐ AAPI ☐ LATINX ☐ ESL ☐ LGBTQ+
CATEGORY / GENRE :

SO... WHAT'D YOU THINK?
☐ NOT MY BAG ☐ JUST OK ☐ TOTALLY RAD!
☐ A REAL SLOG BUT WORTH IT ☐ REPEAT READ FOR SURE ☐ THIS BOOK CHANGED MY LIFE

QUICK SUMMARY / LOGLINE :

QUOTE OR CONCEPT TO REMEMBER :

WHO WOULD YOU RECOMMEND THIS TO :

TITLE : DATE STARTED :
DATE FINISHED :

AUTHOR :
☐ BIPOC ☐ AAPI ☐ LATINX ☐ ESL ☐ LGBTQ+
CATEGORY / GENRE :

SO... WHAT'D YOU THINK?

☐ NOT MY BAG ☐ JUST OK ☐ TOTALLY RAD!
☐ A REAL SLOG BUT WORTH IT ☐ REPEAT READ FOR SURE ☐ THIS BOOK CHANGED MY LIFE

QUICK SUMMARY / LOGLINE :

QUOTE OR CONCEPT TO REMEMBER :

WHO WOULD YOU RECOMMEND THIS TO :

TITLE : DATE STARTED :
　　　　　DATE FINISHED :

AUTHOR :
☐ BIPOC ☐ AAPI ☐ LATINX ☐ ESL ☐ LGBTQ+
CATEGORY / GENRE :

SO... WHAT'D YOU THINK?

☐ NOT MY BAG ☐ JUST OK ☐ TOTALLY RAD!
☐ A REAL SLOG BUT WORTH IT ☐ REPEAT READ FOR SURE ☐ THIS BOOK CHANGED MY LIFE

QUICK SUMMARY / LOGLINE :

QUOTE OR CONCEPT TO REMEMBER :

WHO WOULD YOU RECOMMEND THIS TO :

TITLE :   DATE STARTED :
                                 DATE FINISHED :

AUTHOR :
☐ BIPOC   ☐ AAPI   ☐ LATINX   ☐ ESL   ☐ LGBTQ+
CATEGORY / GENRE :

SO... WHAT'D YOU THINK?

☐ NOT MY BAG   ☐ JUST OK   ☐ TOTALLY RAD!
☐ A REAL SLOG   ☐ REPEAT READ   ☐ THIS BOOK CHANGED
  BUT WORTH IT   FOR SURE   MY LIFE

QUICK SUMMARY / LOGLINE :

QUOTE OR CONCEPT TO REMEMBER :

WHO WOULD YOU RECOMMEND THIS TO :

TITLE :　　　　　　　　　　　　DATE STARTED :
　　　　　　　　　　　　　　　　DATE FINISHED :

AUTHOR :
☐ BIPOC　☐ AAPI　☐ LATINX　☐ ESL　☐ LGBTQ+

CATEGORY / GENRE :

SO... WHAT'D YOU THINK?

☐ NOT MY BAG　☐ JUST OK　☐ TOTALLY RAD!

☐ A REAL SLOG　☐ REPEAT READ　☐ THIS BOOK CHANGED
　 BUT WORTH IT　　 FOR SURE　　　　 MY LIFE

QUICK SUMMARY / LOGLINE :

QUOTE OR CONCEPT TO REMEMBER :

WHO WOULD YOU RECOMMEND THIS TO :

TITLE : DATE STARTED :
         DATE FINISHED :

AUTHOR :
☐ BIPOC ☐ AAPI ☐ LATINX ☐ ESL ☐ LGBTQ+
CATEGORY / GENRE :

SO... WHAT'D YOU THINK?

☐ NOT MY BAG ☐ JUST OK ☐ TOTALLY RAD!
☐ A REAL SLOG ☐ REPEAT READ ☐ THIS BOOK CHANGED
  BUT WORTH IT   FOR SURE   MY LIFE

QUICK SUMMARY / LOGLINE :

QUOTE OR CONCEPT TO REMEMBER :

WHO WOULD YOU RECOMMEND THIS TO :

TITLE : DATE STARTED :
DATE FINISHED :

AUTHOR :
☐ BIPOC ☐ AAPI ☐ LATINX ☐ ESL ☐ LGBTQ+
CATEGORY / GENRE :

SO... WHAT'D YOU THINK?
☐ NOT MY BAG ☐ JUST OK ☐ TOTALLY RAD!
☐ A REAL SLOG BUT WORTH IT ☐ REPEAT READ FOR SURE ☐ THIS BOOK CHANGED MY LIFE

QUICK SUMMARY / LOGLINE :

QUOTE OR CONCEPT TO REMEMBER :

WHO WOULD YOU RECOMMEND THIS TO :

TITLE : DATE STARTED :
DATE FINISHED :

AUTHOR :

☐ BIPOC ☐ AAPI ☐ LATINX ☐ ESL ☐ LGBTQ+

CATEGORY / GENRE :

SO... WHAT'D YOU THINK?

☐ NOT MY BAG ☐ JUST OK ☐ TOTALLY RAD!

☐ A REAL SLOG BUT WORTH IT ☐ REPEAT READ FOR SURE ☐ THIS BOOK CHANGED MY LIFE

QUICK SUMMARY / LOGLINE :

QUOTE OR CONCEPT TO REMEMBER :

WHO WOULD YOU RECOMMEND THIS TO :

TITLE :   DATE STARTED :
          DATE FINISHED :

AUTHOR :
☐ BIPOC   ☐ AAPI   ☐ LATINX   ☐ ESL   ☐ LGBTQ+
CATEGORY / GENRE :

SO... WHAT'D YOU THINK?

☐ NOT MY BAG   ☐ JUST OK   ☐ TOTALLY RAD!
☐ A REAL SLOG   ☐ REPEAT READ   ☐ THIS BOOK CHANGED
  BUT WORTH IT   FOR SURE   MY LIFE

QUICK SUMMARY / LOGLINE :

QUOTE OR CONCEPT TO REMEMBER :

WHO WOULD YOU RECOMMEND THIS TO :

TITLE : DATE STARTED :
　　　　　DATE FINISHED :

AUTHOR :
☐ BIPOC ☐ AAPI ☐ LATINX ☐ ESL ☐ LGBTQ+
CATEGORY / GENRE :

SO... WHAT'D YOU THINK?

☐ NOT MY BAG ☐ JUST OK ☐ TOTALLY RAD!
☐ A REAL SLOG ☐ REPEAT READ ☐ THIS BOOK CHANGED
　BUT WORTH IT 　FOR SURE 　MY LIFE

QUICK SUMMARY / LOGLINE :

QUOTE OR CONCEPT TO REMEMBER :

WHO WOULD YOU RECOMMEND THIS TO :

TITLE : DATE STARTED :
DATE FINISHED :

AUTHOR :
☐ BIPOC ☐ AAPI ☐ LATINX ☐ ESL ☐ LGBTQ+
CATEGORY / GENRE :

SO... WHAT'D YOU THINK?
☐ NOT MY BAG ☐ JUST OK ☐ TOTALLY RAD!
☐ A REAL SLOG BUT WORTH IT ☐ REPEAT READ FOR SURE ☐ THIS BOOK CHANGED MY LIFE

QUICK SUMMARY / LOGLINE :

QUOTE OR CONCEPT TO REMEMBER :

WHO WOULD YOU RECOMMEND THIS TO :

TITLE :   DATE STARTED :
                                     DATE FINISHED :

AUTHOR :
  ☐ BIPOC   ☐ AAPI   ☐ LATINX   ☐ ESL   ☐ LGBTQ+
CATEGORY / GENRE :

SO... WHAT'D YOU THINK?
  ☐ NOT MY BAG   ☐ JUST OK   ☐ TOTALLY RAD!
  ☐ A REAL SLOG   ☐ REPEAT READ   ☐ THIS BOOK CHANGED
    BUT WORTH IT   FOR SURE   MY LIFE

QUICK SUMMARY / LOGLINE :

QUOTE OR CONCEPT TO REMEMBER :

WHO WOULD YOU RECOMMEND THIS TO :

TITLE :　　　　　　　　　　　　DATE STARTED :
　　　　　　　　　　　　　　　　DATE FINISHED :

AUTHOR :
　☐ BIPOC　☐ AAPI　☐ LATINX　☐ ESL　☐ LGBTQ+
CATEGORY / GENRE :

SO... WHAT'D YOU THINK?

☐ NOT MY BAG　☐ JUST OK　☐ TOTALLY RAD!

☐ A REAL SLOG　☐ REPEAT READ　☐ THIS BOOK CHANGED
　BUT WORTH IT　　FOR SURE　　　MY LIFE

QUICK SUMMARY / LOGLINE :

QUOTE OR CONCEPT TO REMEMBER :

WHO WOULD YOU RECOMMEND THIS TO :

TITLE :

DATE STARTED :
DATE FINISHED :

AUTHOR :

☐ BIPOC ☐ AAPI ☐ LATINX ☐ ESL ☐ LGBTQ+

CATEGORY / GENRE :

SO... WHAT'D YOU THINK?

☐ NOT MY BAG ☐ JUST OK ☐ TOTALLY RAD!
☐ A REAL SLOG BUT WORTH IT ☐ REPEAT READ FOR SURE ☐ THIS BOOK CHANGED MY LIFE

QUICK SUMMARY / LOGLINE :

QUOTE OR CONCEPT TO REMEMBER :

WHO WOULD YOU RECOMMEND THIS TO :

TITLE :

DATE STARTED :
DATE FINISHED :

AUTHOR :
☐ BIPOC ☐ AAPI ☐ LATINX ☐ ESL ☐ LGBTQ+

CATEGORY / GENRE :

SO... WHAT'D YOU THINK?
☐ NOT MY BAG ☐ JUST OK ☐ TOTALLY RAD!
☐ A REAL SLOG BUT WORTH IT ☐ REPEAT READ FOR SURE ☐ THIS BOOK CHANGED MY LIFE

QUICK SUMMARY / LOGLINE :

QUOTE OR CONCEPT TO REMEMBER :

WHO WOULD YOU RECOMMEND THIS TO :

TITLE :   DATE STARTED :
                               DATE FINISHED :

AUTHOR :
☐ BIPOC   ☐ AAPI   ☐ LATINX   ☐ ESL   ☐ LGBTQ+
CATEGORY / GENRE :

SO... WHAT'D YOU THINK?

☐ NOT MY BAG   ☐ JUST OK   ☐ TOTALLY RAD!
☐ A REAL SLOG   ☐ REPEAT READ   ☐ THIS BOOK CHANGED
  BUT WORTH IT   FOR SURE   MY LIFE

QUICK SUMMARY / LOGLINE :

QUOTE OR CONCEPT TO REMEMBER :

WHO WOULD YOU RECOMMEND THIS TO :

TITLE :   DATE STARTED :
                                     DATE FINISHED :

AUTHOR :
 ☐ BIPOC   ☐ AAPI   ☐ LATINX   ☐ ESL   ☐ LGBTQ+
CATEGORY / GENRE :

SO... WHAT'D YOU THINK?
☐ NOT MY BAG   ☐ JUST OK   ☐ TOTALLY RAD!
☐ A REAL SLOG   ☐ REPEAT READ   ☐ THIS BOOK CHANGED
  BUT WORTH IT   FOR SURE   MY LIFE

QUICK SUMMARY / LOGLINE :

QUOTE OR CONCEPT TO REMEMBER :

WHO WOULD YOU RECOMMEND THIS TO :

TITLE : DATE STARTED :
DATE FINISHED :

AUTHOR :
☐ BIPOC ☐ AAPI ☐ LATINX ☐ ESL ☐ LGBTQ+
CATEGORY / GENRE :

SO... WHAT'D YOU THINK?
☐ NOT MY BAG ☐ JUST OK ☐ TOTALLY RAD!
☐ A REAL SLOG BUT WORTH IT ☐ REPEAT READ FOR SURE ☐ THIS BOOK CHANGED MY LIFE

QUICK SUMMARY / LOGLINE :

QUOTE OR CONCEPT TO REMEMBER :

WHO WOULD YOU RECOMMEND THIS TO :

TITLE :　　　　　　　　　　　DATE STARTED :
　　　　　　　　　　　　　　DATE FINISHED :

AUTHOR :
☐ BIPOC　☐ AAPI　☐ LATINX　☐ ESL　☐ LGBTQ+
CATEGORY / GENRE :

SO... WHAT'D YOU THINK?

☐ NOT MY BAG　☐ JUST OK　☐ TOTALLY RAD!
☐ A REAL SLOG BUT WORTH IT　☐ REPEAT READ FOR SURE　☐ THIS BOOK CHANGED MY LIFE

QUICK SUMMARY / LOGLINE :

QUOTE OR CONCEPT TO REMEMBER :

WHO WOULD YOU RECOMMEND THIS TO :

TITLE :　　　　　　　　　　　　DATE STARTED :
　　　　　　　　　　　　　　　　DATE FINISHED :

AUTHOR :
☐ BIPOC　☐ AAPI　☐ LATINX　☐ ESL　☐ LGBTQ+
CATEGORY / GENRE :

SO... WHAT'D YOU THINK?

☐ NOT MY BAG　☐ JUST OK　☐ TOTALLY RAD!
☐ A REAL SLOG　☐ REPEAT READ　☐ THIS BOOK CHANGED
　　BUT WORTH IT　　FOR SURE　　　MY LIFE

QUICK SUMMARY / LOGLINE :

QUOTE OR CONCEPT TO REMEMBER :

WHO WOULD YOU RECOMMEND THIS TO :

TITLE :   DATE STARTED :
                                 DATE FINISHED :

AUTHOR :
☐ BIPOC   ☐ AAPI   ☐ LATINX   ☐ ESL   ☐ LGBTQ+
CATEGORY / GENRE :

SO... WHAT'D YOU THINK?

☐ NOT MY BAG   ☐ JUST OK   ☐ TOTALLY RAD!
☐ A REAL SLOG   ☐ REPEAT READ   ☐ THIS BOOK CHANGED
  BUT WORTH IT   FOR SURE   MY LIFE

QUICK SUMMARY / LOGLINE :

QUOTE OR CONCEPT TO REMEMBER :

WHO WOULD YOU RECOMMEND THIS TO :

TITLE : DATE STARTED :
DATE FINISHED :

AUTHOR :
☐ BIPOC ☐ AAPI ☐ LATINX ☐ ESL ☐ LGBTQ+
CATEGORY / GENRE :

SO... WHAT'D YOU THINK?
☐ NOT MY BAG ☐ JUST OK ☐ TOTALLY RAD!
☐ A REAL SLOG BUT WORTH IT ☐ REPEAT READ FOR SURE ☐ THIS BOOK CHANGED MY LIFE

QUICK SUMMARY / LOGLINE :

QUOTE OR CONCEPT TO REMEMBER :

WHO WOULD YOU RECOMMEND THIS TO :

TITLE :　　　　　　　　　　DATE STARTED :
　　　　　　　　　　　　　　DATE FINISHED :

AUTHOR :
☐ BIPOC　☐ AAPI　☐ LATINX　☐ ESL　☐ LGBTQ+
CATEGORY / GENRE :

SO... WHAT'D YOU THINK?
☐ NOT MY BAG　☐ JUST OK　☐ TOTALLY RAD!
☐ A REAL SLOG BUT WORTH IT　☐ REPEAT READ FOR SURE　☐ THIS BOOK CHANGED MY LIFE

QUICK SUMMARY / LOGLINE :

QUOTE OR CONCEPT TO REMEMBER :

WHO WOULD YOU RECOMMEND THIS TO :

TITLE :
DATE STARTED :
DATE FINISHED :

AUTHOR :
☐ BIPOC ☐ AAPI ☐ LATINX ☐ ESL ☐ LGBTQ+
CATEGORY / GENRE :

SO... WHAT'D YOU THINK?
☐ NOT MY BAG ☐ JUST OK ☐ TOTALLY RAD!
☐ A REAL SLOG BUT WORTH IT ☐ REPEAT READ FOR SURE ☐ THIS BOOK CHANGED MY LIFE

QUICK SUMMARY / LOGLINE :

QUOTE OR CONCEPT TO REMEMBER :

WHO WOULD YOU RECOMMEND THIS TO :

TITLE :   DATE STARTED :
                                           DATE FINISHED :

AUTHOR :
  ☐ BIPOC   ☐ AAPI   ☐ LATINX   ☐ ESL   ☐ LGBTQ+
CATEGORY / GENRE :

SO... WHAT'D YOU THINK?

☐ NOT MY BAG   ☐ JUST OK   ☐ TOTALLY RAD!
☐ A REAL SLOG   ☐ REPEAT READ   ☐ THIS BOOK CHANGED
  BUT WORTH IT   FOR SURE   MY LIFE

QUICK SUMMARY / LOGLINE :

QUOTE OR CONCEPT TO REMEMBER :

WHO WOULD YOU RECOMMEND THIS TO :

TITLE :
DATE STARTED :
DATE FINISHED :

AUTHOR :
☐ BIPOC ☐ AAPI ☐ LATINX ☐ ESL ☐ LGBTQ+
CATEGORY / GENRE :

SO... WHAT'D YOU THINK?
☐ NOT MY BAG ☐ JUST OK ☐ TOTALLY RAD!
☐ A REAL SLOG BUT WORTH IT ☐ REPEAT READ FOR SURE ☐ THIS BOOK CHANGED MY LIFE

QUICK SUMMARY / LOGLINE :

QUOTE OR CONCEPT TO REMEMBER :

WHO WOULD YOU RECOMMEND THIS TO :

TITLE :   DATE STARTED :
                                  DATE FINISHED :

AUTHOR :
  ☐ BIPOC   ☐ AAPI   ☐ LATINX   ☐ ESL   ☐ LGBTQ+
CATEGORY / GENRE :

SO... WHAT'D YOU THINK?
  ☐ NOT MY BAG   ☐ JUST OK   ☐ TOTALLY RAD!
  ☐ A REAL SLOG   ☐ REPEAT READ   ☐ THIS BOOK CHANGED
    BUT WORTH IT   FOR SURE   MY LIFE

QUICK SUMMARY / LOGLINE :

QUOTE OR CONCEPT TO REMEMBER :

WHO WOULD YOU RECOMMEND THIS TO :

TITLE :
DATE STARTED :
DATE FINISHED :

AUTHOR :
☐ BIPOC ☐ AAPI ☐ LATINX ☐ ESL ☐ LGBTQ+
CATEGORY / GENRE :

SO... WHAT'D YOU THINK?
☐ NOT MY BAG ☐ JUST OK ☐ TOTALLY RAD!
☐ A REAL SLOG BUT WORTH IT ☐ REPEAT READ FOR SURE ☐ THIS BOOK CHANGED MY LIFE

QUICK SUMMARY / LOGLINE :

QUOTE OR CONCEPT TO REMEMBER :

WHO WOULD YOU RECOMMEND THIS TO :

TITLE : DATE STARTED :
 DATE FINISHED :

AUTHOR :
☐ BIPOC ☐ AAPI ☐ LATINX ☐ ESL ☐ LGBTQ+
CATEGORY / GENRE :

SO... WHAT'D YOU THINK?
☐ NOT MY BAG ☐ JUST OK ☐ TOTALLY RAD!
☐ A REAL SLOG BUT WORTH IT ☐ REPEAT READ FOR SURE ☐ THIS BOOK CHANGED MY LIFE

QUICK SUMMARY / LOGLINE :

QUOTE OR CONCEPT TO REMEMBER :

WHO WOULD YOU RECOMMEND THIS TO :

TITLE :

DATE STARTED :

DATE FINISHED :

AUTHOR :

☐ BIPOC ☐ AAPI ☐ LATINX ☐ ESL ☐ LGBTQ+

CATEGORY / GENRE :

SO... WHAT'D YOU THINK?

☐ NOT MY BAG ☐ JUST OK ☐ TOTALLY RAD!

☐ A REAL SLOG BUT WORTH IT ☐ REPEAT READ FOR SURE ☐ THIS BOOK CHANGED MY LIFE

QUICK SUMMARY / LOGLINE :

QUOTE OR CONCEPT TO REMEMBER :

WHO WOULD YOU RECOMMEND THIS TO :

TITLE :   DATE STARTED :
          DATE FINISHED :

AUTHOR :
☐ BIPOC   ☐ AAPI   ☐ LATINX   ☐ ESL   ☐ LGBTQ+
CATEGORY / GENRE :

SO... WHAT'D YOU THINK?

☐ NOT MY BAG   ☐ JUST OK   ☐ TOTALLY RAD!
☐ A REAL SLOG   ☐ REPEAT READ   ☐ THIS BOOK CHANGED
  BUT WORTH IT   FOR SURE   MY LIFE

QUICK SUMMARY / LOGLINE :

QUOTE OR CONCEPT TO REMEMBER :

WHO WOULD YOU RECOMMEND THIS TO :

TITLE :

DATE STARTED :
DATE FINISHED :

AUTHOR :

☐ BIPOC ☐ AAPI ☐ LATINX ☐ ESL ☐ LGBTQ+

CATEGORY / GENRE :

SO... WHAT'D YOU THINK?

☐ NOT MY BAG ☐ JUST OK ☐ TOTALLY RAD!
☐ A REAL SLOG BUT WORTH IT ☐ REPEAT READ FOR SURE ☐ THIS BOOK CHANGED MY LIFE

QUICK SUMMARY / LOGLINE :

QUOTE OR CONCEPT TO REMEMBER :

WHO WOULD YOU RECOMMEND THIS TO :

TITLE : DATE STARTED :
DATE FINISHED :

AUTHOR :
☐ BIPOC ☐ AAPI ☐ LATINX ☐ ESL ☐ LGBTQ+
CATEGORY / GENRE :

SO... WHAT'D YOU THINK?
☐ NOT MY BAG ☐ JUST OK ☐ TOTALLY RAD!
☐ A REAL SLOG BUT WORTH IT ☐ REPEAT READ FOR SURE ☐ THIS BOOK CHANGED MY LIFE

QUICK SUMMARY / LOGLINE :

QUOTE OR CONCEPT TO REMEMBER :

WHO WOULD YOU RECOMMEND THIS TO :

TITLE : DATE STARTED :
DATE FINISHED :

AUTHOR :
☐ BIPOC ☐ AAPI ☐ LATINX ☐ ESL ☐ LGBTQ+
CATEGORY / GENRE :

SO... WHAT'D YOU THINK?
☐ NOT MY BAG ☐ JUST OK ☐ TOTALLY RAD!
☐ A REAL SLOG BUT WORTH IT ☐ REPEAT READ FOR SURE ☐ THIS BOOK CHANGED MY LIFE

QUICK SUMMARY / LOGLINE :

QUOTE OR CONCEPT TO REMEMBER :

WHO WOULD YOU RECOMMEND THIS TO :

TITLE :   DATE STARTED :
                                    DATE FINISHED :

AUTHOR :
☐ BIPOC   ☐ AAPI   ☐ LATINX   ☐ ESL   ☐ LGBTQ+
CATEGORY / GENRE :

SO... WHAT'D YOU THINK?

☐ NOT MY BAG   ☐ JUST OK   ☐ TOTALLY RAD!
☐ A REAL SLOG   ☐ REPEAT READ   ☐ THIS BOOK CHANGED
  BUT WORTH IT   FOR SURE   MY LIFE

QUICK SUMMARY / LOGLINE :

QUOTE OR CONCEPT TO REMEMBER :

WHO WOULD YOU RECOMMEND THIS TO :

TITLE :   DATE STARTED :
                                     DATE FINISHED :

AUTHOR :
☐ BIPOC   ☐ AAPI   ☐ LATINX   ☐ ESL   ☐ LGBTQ+
CATEGORY / GENRE :

SO... WHAT'D YOU THINK?

☐ NOT MY BAG   ☐ JUST OK   ☐ TOTALLY RAD!
☐ A REAL SLOG   ☐ REPEAT READ   ☐ THIS BOOK CHANGED
  BUT WORTH IT   FOR SURE   MY LIFE

QUICK SUMMARY / LOGLINE :

QUOTE OR CONCEPT TO REMEMBER :

WHO WOULD YOU RECOMMEND THIS TO :

TITLE : DATE STARTED :
DATE FINISHED :

AUTHOR :
☐ BIPOC ☐ AAPI ☐ LATINX ☐ ESL ☐ LGBTQ+
CATEGORY / GENRE :

SO... WHAT'D YOU THINK?
☐ NOT MY BAG ☐ JUST OK ☐ TOTALLY RAD!
☐ A REAL SLOG BUT WORTH IT ☐ REPEAT READ FOR SURE ☐ THIS BOOK CHANGED MY LIFE

QUICK SUMMARY / LOGLINE :

QUOTE OR CONCEPT TO REMEMBER :

WHO WOULD YOU RECOMMEND THIS TO :

TITLE :   DATE STARTED :
                                     DATE FINISHED :

AUTHOR :
  ☐ BIPOC   ☐ AAPI   ☐ LATINX   ☐ ESL   ☐ LGBTQ+
CATEGORY / GENRE :

SO... WHAT'D YOU THINK?
  ☐ NOT MY BAG   ☐ JUST OK   ☐ TOTALLY RAD!
  ☐ A REAL SLOG   ☐ REPEAT READ   ☐ THIS BOOK CHANGED
    BUT WORTH IT   FOR SURE   MY LIFE

QUICK SUMMARY / LOGLINE :

QUOTE OR CONCEPT TO REMEMBER :

WHO WOULD YOU RECOMMEND THIS TO :

TITLE :   DATE STARTED :
                                 DATE FINISHED :

AUTHOR :
  ☐ BIPOC   ☐ AAPI   ☐ LATINX   ☐ ESL   ☐ LGBTQ+
CATEGORY / GENRE :

SO... WHAT'D YOU THINK?
  ☐ NOT MY BAG   ☐ JUST OK   ☐ TOTALLY RAD!
  ☐ A REAL SLOG   ☐ REPEAT READ   ☐ THIS BOOK CHANGED
     BUT WORTH IT   FOR SURE   MY LIFE

QUICK SUMMARY / LOGLINE :

QUOTE OR CONCEPT TO REMEMBER :

WHO WOULD YOU RECOMMEND THIS TO :

TITLE :
DATE STARTED :
DATE FINISHED :

AUTHOR :
☐ BIPOC ☐ AAPI ☐ LATINX ☐ ESL ☐ LGBTQ+
CATEGORY / GENRE :

SO... WHAT'D YOU THINK?
☐ NOT MY BAG ☐ JUST OK ☐ TOTALLY RAD!
☐ A REAL SLOG BUT WORTH IT ☐ REPEAT READ FOR SURE ☐ THIS BOOK CHANGED MY LIFE

QUICK SUMMARY / LOGLINE :

QUOTE OR CONCEPT TO REMEMBER :

WHO WOULD YOU RECOMMEND THIS TO :

TITLE :   DATE STARTED :
           DATE FINISHED :

AUTHOR :
☐ BIPOC   ☐ AAPI   ☐ LATINX   ☐ ESL   ☐ LGBTQ+
CATEGORY / GENRE :

SO... WHAT'D YOU THINK?

☐ NOT MY BAG   ☐ JUST OK   ☐ TOTALLY RAD!
☐ A REAL SLOG   ☐ REPEAT READ   ☐ THIS BOOK CHANGED
  BUT WORTH IT   FOR SURE   MY LIFE

QUICK SUMMARY / LOGLINE :

QUOTE OR CONCEPT TO REMEMBER :

WHO WOULD YOU RECOMMEND THIS TO :

TITLE :　　　　　　　　　　　　DATE STARTED :
　　　　　　　　　　　　　　　　DATE FINISHED :

AUTHOR :
☐ BIPOC　☐ AAPI　☐ LATINX　☐ ESL　☐ LGBTQ+
CATEGORY / GENRE :

SO... WHAT'D YOU THINK?

☐ NOT MY BAG　☐ JUST OK　☐ TOTALLY RAD!
☐ A REAL SLOG　☐ REPEAT READ　☐ THIS BOOK CHANGED
　 BUT WORTH IT　　FOR SURE　　　MY LIFE

QUICK SUMMARY / LOGLINE :

QUOTE OR CONCEPT TO REMEMBER :

WHO WOULD YOU RECOMMEND THIS TO :

TITLE :   DATE STARTED :
                                  DATE FINISHED :

AUTHOR :
☐ BIPOC   ☐ AAPI   ☐ LATINX   ☐ ESL   ☐ LGBTQ+
CATEGORY / GENRE :

SO... WHAT'D YOU THINK?

☐ NOT MY BAG   ☐ JUST OK   ☐ TOTALLY RAD!
☐ A REAL SLOG   ☐ REPEAT READ   ☐ THIS BOOK CHANGED
  BUT WORTH IT   FOR SURE   MY LIFE

QUICK SUMMARY / LOGLINE :

QUOTE OR CONCEPT TO REMEMBER :

WHO WOULD YOU RECOMMEND THIS TO :

TITLE :   DATE STARTED :
                      DATE FINISHED :

AUTHOR :
  ☐ BIPOC   ☐ AAPI   ☐ LATINX   ☐ ESL   ☐ LGBTQ+
CATEGORY / GENRE :

SO... WHAT'D YOU THINK?
☐ NOT MY BAG   ☐ JUST OK   ☐ TOTALLY RAD!
☐ A REAL SLOG   ☐ REPEAT READ   ☐ THIS BOOK CHANGED
  BUT WORTH IT   FOR SURE   MY LIFE

QUICK SUMMARY / LOGLINE :

QUOTE OR CONCEPT TO REMEMBER :

WHO WOULD YOU RECOMMEND THIS TO :

TITLE : DATE STARTED :
DATE FINISHED :

AUTHOR :
☐ BIPOC ☐ AAPI ☐ LATINX ☐ ESL ☐ LGBTQ+
CATEGORY / GENRE :

SO... WHAT'D YOU THINK?
☐ NOT MY BAG ☐ JUST OK ☐ TOTALLY RAD!
☐ A REAL SLOG BUT WORTH IT ☐ REPEAT READ FOR SURE ☐ THIS BOOK CHANGED MY LIFE

QUICK SUMMARY / LOGLINE :

QUOTE OR CONCEPT TO REMEMBER :

WHO WOULD YOU RECOMMEND THIS TO :

TITLE :　　　　　　　　　　　DATE STARTED :
　　　　　　　　　　　　　　　DATE FINISHED :

AUTHOR :
☐ BIPOC　☐ AAPI　☐ LATINX　☐ ESL　☐ LGBTQ+

CATEGORY / GENRE :

SO... WHAT'D YOU THINK?

☐ NOT MY BAG　☐ JUST OK　☐ TOTALLY RAD!

☐ A REAL SLOG BUT WORTH IT　☐ REPEAT READ FOR SURE　☐ THIS BOOK CHANGED MY LIFE

QUICK SUMMARY / LOGLINE :

QUOTE OR CONCEPT TO REMEMBER :

WHO WOULD YOU RECOMMEND THIS TO :

TITLE : DATE STARTED :
DATE FINISHED :

AUTHOR :
☐ BIPOC ☐ AAPI ☐ LATINX ☐ ESL ☐ LGBTQ+
CATEGORY / GENRE :

SO... WHAT'D YOU THINK?
☐ NOT MY BAG ☐ JUST OK ☐ TOTALLY RAD!
☐ A REAL SLOG BUT WORTH IT ☐ REPEAT READ FOR SURE ☐ THIS BOOK CHANGED MY LIFE

QUICK SUMMARY / LOGLINE :

QUOTE OR CONCEPT TO REMEMBER :

WHO WOULD YOU RECOMMEND THIS TO :

TITLE :   DATE STARTED :
                                 DATE FINISHED :

AUTHOR :
  ☐ BIPOC   ☐ AAPI   ☐ LATINX   ☐ ESL   ☐ LGBTQ+
CATEGORY / GENRE :

SO... WHAT'D YOU THINK?

☐ NOT MY BAG   ☐ JUST OK   ☐ TOTALLY RAD!
☐ A REAL SLOG   ☐ REPEAT READ   ☐ THIS BOOK CHANGED
  BUT WORTH IT   FOR SURE   MY LIFE

QUICK SUMMARY / LOGLINE :

QUOTE OR CONCEPT TO REMEMBER :

WHO WOULD YOU RECOMMEND THIS TO :

TITLE :

DATE STARTED :
DATE FINISHED :

AUTHOR :

☐ BIPOC ☐ AAPI ☐ LATINX ☐ ESL ☐ LGBTQ+

CATEGORY / GENRE :

SO... WHAT'D YOU THINK?

☐ NOT MY BAG ☐ JUST OK ☐ TOTALLY RAD!
☐ A REAL SLOG BUT WORTH IT ☐ REPEAT READ FOR SURE ☐ THIS BOOK CHANGED MY LIFE

QUICK SUMMARY / LOGLINE :

QUOTE OR CONCEPT TO REMEMBER :

WHO WOULD YOU RECOMMEND THIS TO :

CPSIA information can be obtained
at www.ICGtesting.com
Printed in the USA
LVHW052256101121
702990LV00021B/354